6/12

Shorewood – Troy Library
650 Deerwood Drive
Shorewood, IL 60404
815-725-1715

Farm Machines

Tractors

Connor Dayton

PowerKiDS press.

New York

Published in 2012 by The Rosen Publishing Group, Inc.
29 East 21st Street, New York, NY 10010

First Edition

Editor: Jennifer Way
Designer: Greg Tucker

Photo Credits: Cover, pp. 4–5, 7, 9, 10–11, 14–15, 18–19, 21, 23, 24 (top right, top left, bottom left) Shutterstock.com; p. 13 Digital Vision/Valueline/Thinkstock; pp. 16–17 Hemera/Thinkstock; p. 24 (bottom right) Thinkstock Images/Comstock/Thinkstock.

Library of Congress Cataloging-in-Publication Data

Dayton, Connor.
 Tractors / by Connor Dayton. — 1st ed.
    p. cm. — (Farm machines)
 Includes index.
 ISBN 978-1-4488-4946-8 (library binding) — ISBN 978-1-4488-5042-6 (pbk.) —
 ISBN 978-1-4488-5043-3 (6-pack)
 1. Tractors—Juvenile literature. I. Title.
 TL233.15.D73 2012
 631.3'72—dc22
                                            2010048083

Manufactured in the United States of America

CPSIA Compliance Information: Batch #WS11PK: For Further Information contact Rosen Publishing, New York, New York at 1-800-237-9932

Contents

Tractors are hardworking
farm machines.

Tractors come in
many sizes.

Tractor tires have **grooves**. They keep the tractor from sliding in the mud.

The **steering wheel** is in the tractor's **cab**.

Tractors have two brakes. There is one for each back wheel.

The brakes help
the tractor make
sharp turns.

A tractor's back wheels are bigger than its front wheels.

The cab's frame must be strong to protect the farmer.

A tractor's main job is pulling farming tools. Tractors can pull **plows**.

Tractors help farmers
all over their farms!

Words to Know

cab

grooves

plow

steering wheel

Index

Web Sites

Due to the changing nature of Internet links, PowerKids Press has developed an online list of Web sites related to the subject of this book. This site is updated regularly. Please use this link to access the list:
www.powerkidslinks.com/farm/tractors/